Have a Magical Day

7 Keys to Living Happy Every Day

By: Wendell Miracle

Copyrights © 2020 - Hope Nuggets LLC

Disclaimer

The copyrights of this content belong to the Author and Hope Nuggets

LLC

The information contained in the book and its related guides are deemed to serve as a part of the author's collection of books, which may increase their revenue and income passively. The tips, strategies, tricks, and the information in this book take no guarantee that someone else's research will also produce results synonymous to it. The material can include content or information from the third party, but the author takes full charge of quoting genuine resources that may be subjected to copyright issues.

The author takes no charge of the opinion that any of the third-party or unrelated individuals have. If the content inculcated in the publication becomes obsolete due to technical reasons or whatsoever, the author or the publication house are entitled to no blames. All of the events indicated in the book are the result of primary research, secondary research, and the personal experience of the person(s) involved in formulating the book and bringing it into the form it is in today. All the content used in this book belongs solely to the author. No part of this shall be reproduced, sold, or transmitted in any medium by the third party except after the author's approval.

Acknowledgements

I Dedicate this book to each and every one of you. To every single person who's been following us on social media through the years and the people who just recently found out about us.

From the bottom of my heart I want to say Thank you! This book wouldn't be possible without all your support. You have changed my life! And I sincerely hope this book changes yours.

Thank you to my amazing editors and publishers for helping us complete this project.

Thank you for all the people in my life who pushed me to do this. I never realized how difficult it would be to write a book until I went through the process.

I never imagined it would take three years to fully complete this, but it has been absolutely worth it.

And finally, a big thank you to my mother in Heaven. Mom, this is for you. Thank you for being my greatest source of strength and inspiration.

Contents

Disclaimer I

Acknowledgements II

Introduction 1

Chapter 1: Begin each day with Gratitude 6

Chapter 2: Be a Blessing 31

Chapter 3: Visualize your Success 47

Chapter 4: Forgive Others 64

Chapter 5: Love Yourself 72

Chapter 6: Speak it into your Existence 84

Chapter 7: Dance like You Already Got It 90

About the Author 105

~Have a Magical Day~

Introduction

When you tell people to have a 'Magical Day,' they think you're referring to Disney Land. However, you can't really blame them. They call that venue the 'happiest place on earth.' People go there and pay top dollar to experience joy and bliss for a few hours. Folks often drive hours and fly across the country to get their happiness fix. People usually go there to relieve stress and anxiety.

But why not feel joy and bliss every single day? Why not go to work and experience magic? Why not live every day with the same excitement you would have as if you were going to Disney Land?

~Have a Magical Day~

The truth is, You *Can* live this type of life. You *can* live each day without so much worry, stress, and anxiety, and you *can* accomplish your goals and dreams.

Come with me on this journey to find what billions of people in the world strive to find – Happiness. Trust me, it's a lot easier than you think.

I used to live my life on autopilot. I would just let things happen and let things be. If something good happened, I would say I got a lucky break. If something bad happened, I would conjure up reasons as to why, without ever having a real revelation of why. For years, I lived a vicious cycle of good days and bad days, happy days and depressed days, exciting days and boring days. However, the problem was, the happy, exciting, and

~Have a Magical Day~

magical days didn't happen as frequently as I would have liked.

One day, I told myself, enough is enough. I want to be happy every day. I want to experience joy and happiness daily, not just on weekends or special events like weddings, graduations, and family vacations.

So I did research; Tons of research. I studied the lives of those who were not only successful financially, but in every area of their lives — body, soul, and mind. One of the main common denominators that I found was that their daily routine and their daily practices were a huge reason as to why they were successful.

Then I decided to try them out for myself to see if they worked. They sure did! I went from living with

~Have a Magical Day~

very little energy to having amazing energy all throughout the day (without drinking 6 cups of coffee or 4 rock star energy drinks). I went from living check to check to having an abundance.

I went from having 'blah' feelings all day to feeling an unexplainable joy throughout my day. Also, I transformed my life from a life of anxiety and worry into a life of peace and serenity.

I wrote this book to share with you the things I do in my daily routine that have led to tremendous success in every area of my life!

When you follow the seven simple principles found in this book, you will wake up every morning so excited to be alive. You will feel like you're floating on

~Have a Magical Day~

air, and everything you desire will manifest in your life.

Every day will be downright *Magical*.

1

Chapter 1: Begin each day with Gratitude

Every morning I wake up, and I thank God for two precious gifts: my eyes. I thank Him for a heart that beats and the fact that I'm alive to see another day.

I thank Him for the magical air that I breathe. I'm grateful that when I tell my hands to move, they move; when I tell my feet to walk, they obey. My friends, the way you start your day determines the type of day you are going to have.

One of my favorite Psalms in the Bible is chapter 100:4, which says, "Enter His gates with thanksgiving and into his courts with praise." I've come to the realization that when I start my day thanking God, it goes so much better. Yes, I have some prayer requests. Yes, I have some problems. Yes, I have some unresolved issues. However, one of my first prayers is, "Thank you God for another day. Thank you that I'm alive. Thank you that I'm not in a hospital somewhere."

If you woke up and you can see, hear, walk, and talk, then you're rich. If you're able to see your significant other, your children, or your pets, you're wealthy. Our relationships are what make our lives meaningful and fulfilling, and you ought to give thanks for them.

"Let everything that has breath praise the Lord"

Psalm 150:6

~Have a Magical Day~

If you can breathe without any issues, you have a reason to rejoice and give thanks. Instead of using your breath to complain and be negative, use that same breath to be grateful for the gift of life!

Sometimes, we take things for granted because we can't see them. You can't see the fact that your heart beats and pumps gallons of blood throughout your body without fail countless times throughout the day. When was the last time you gave thanks for your heart?

Repeat after me, "God, Thank You for my heart."

Studies have shown that you cannot be sad and grateful at the same time. It's literally impossible. Go ahead, try it right now. Try thinking about the greatest day and moment of your life while also simultaneously

~Have a Magical Day~

reliving a traumatizing experience from your past. It can't be done.

Fear, worry, doubt, stress, and anxiety cannot exist when you are in a constant state of gratitude. Gratitude literally eliminates all those other negative emotions and vibrations.

Have you ever noticed that when you start your day grumpy or in a bad mood that all sorts of unfortunate events occur? You stub your toe. You spill your coffee on your white shirt. Every single traffic light is red. You end up being late for work or school, and everything spirals downward. You also end up attracting into your life a bunch of negative people and circumstances.

~Have a Magical Day~

Then again, you have those days where you start off happy and in an amazing mood. You drive into every green light. The day at work and/or school is fun and effortless. You close a big sale. You get the item you wanted at the store discounted, and everyone you run into seems to be happy too. Parking spots open up for you like Moses parting the Red Sea. Every machine at the gym is free, and there's no wait time. The day just has a natural flow to it. You don't feel worried and anxious. You feel an overwhelming sense of joy. It almost feels as though the universe is rigged in your favor. It's an amazing feeling!

This is not a coincidence. The universe operates with specific laws. We obviously know the law of gravity.

~Have a Magical Day~

It doesn't matter if you're a good person or not. What goes up must come down. Another law that is always in operation is the one which states that whatever you give out comes back to you.

Some call it karma. Others call it sowing and reaping. Regardless of the terminology you use, just know it exists. When you give out negative feelings and emotions, you must receive back circumstances, people, and events that cause you to feel negative continuously.

When you radiate good feelings of joy and happiness, you must receive events that cause you to continue to feel those positive emotions. Newton's third law states that "every action has an equal or opposite reaction." So that means that every action of giving thanks

~Have a Magical Day~

will cause a reaction of receiving more things to be thankful for!

You need to make feeling good and happy a top priority in your life! Decide every morning that you're going to be in a good mood! There's no better way to raise your vibrational level of happiness than with gratitude.

So whenever I start my day, I always give thanks for all that I have. My mom taught me when I was younger to count my blessings. It's not just a mundane routine. It's one of the most powerful things that you can do.

"Better to lose count while naming your blessings than to lose your blessings to counting your troubles." – Maltbie D. Babcock

~Have a Magical Day~

Upon rising, you should give thanks for at least ten blessings. This comprised mental list is a lot easier to develop than you think. You can give thanks for the fact that you are alive, the sun that shines bright, and trees that give off oxygen.

You can be grateful for the fact that you have vision and all your five senses. You can express gratitude for the fact that you have a job, a car, and a means to provide for your family.

Speaking of family, be grateful for your loved ones, your kids, your beautiful spouse, and your pets. They bring so much joy and meaning to your life.

~Have a Magical Day~

When you give thanks for your blessings, they multiply! The opposite of gratitude is what so many people do unintentionally, which is to complain.

People complain about the weather, traffic, and their jobs. When you complain, you end up having more to complain about. Similarly, when you are thankful, you end up having more to give thanks for!

'Be thankful for what you have; you'll end up having more. If you concentrate on what you don't have, you will never, ever have enough'. –Oprah Winfrey-

Be thankful for every single part of your morning routine. When I open my eyes, I'm grateful that I get to live to see another day! I'm thankful that God woke me up again! As I walk to my bathroom, I give thanks for

~Have a Magical Day~

running water and for toothpaste, and for the bed I just slept on. I'm grateful for my home, the coffee I drink, and the food on the table. You don't have to limit yourself to just ten blessings. Ten is a good starting point, but to really feel amazing, you can keep adding more to your list! I encourage you all to add ten blessings to your list every day for the next few weeks. Also remember, this doesn't have to take long. You can do this in as little as three minutes, but the difference it can make in your day is incredible.

People may tell me, 'But Wendell, I don't have time to meditate and give thanks.'

If you have time to rush to Starbucks for that Venti mocha, you have time to be grateful. If you have

~Have a Magical Day~

time to watch the news, which will more than likely put you in a not so good mood, you have time to give thanks. If you have time to check Facebook, Instagram, and Snapchat and TikTok right when you wake up, you definitely have the time to give thanks.

As you make gratitude a top priority, you will realize that you have so much to be thankful for! You'll be so grateful that you won't have any time to feel sad!

As you do this consistently, don't be surprised when you notice your days have a special flow. Don't be surprised when you get what other people will consider 'lucky breaks.' These don't happen by accident. They happen through a concentrated effort of practicing gratitude!

~Have a Magical Day~

Why do they say 'practice gratitude'? Because nobody ever wakes up naturally grateful. There's not a single person I know that doesn't wake up grumpy and doesn't go to bed with at least a little bit of anxiety. That's why we have to take action and practice it.

Another excuse people use to not practice gratitude is that they're going through some struggles. This is actually the most opportune time to be grateful! Practicing gratitude in times of trouble allows you to witness a turnaround!

Even if you are currently struggling in certain areas in your life, like your finances, health, or relationships, there is always something to be grateful for.

~Have a Magical Day~

When you look for the good in every situation, the situation must change in your favor!

"If we will be quiet and ready enough, we shall find compensation in every disappointment."

–Henry David Thoreau-

We all experience significant problems in our lives. I've learned that life isn't about the absence of problems, it's about the presence of God's power in the midst of those problems. It's about how we respond to those issues that determine how long we have to endure them.

Life isn't about avoiding the wind and the waves, it's about controlling the condition of your heart and mind during those storms. If you're not experiencing problems,

~Have a Magical Day~

you're either dead, or you're doing absolutely nothing with your life, and that alone is a huge problem.

Have you ever noticed that two people can be going through the exact same problem or storm, yet one person is doing it with faith and courage and with a smile on their face while the other one is dragging through life barely making it? It's all about perspective and how you view your problems. The greatest perspective to have during trying times is gratitude!

"If you change the way you look at things, the things you look at change." –Wayne Dyer-

Let me take this to a whole different level. Back in 2012, after suffering from breast cancer for 13 years, my mother passed away. It was the darkest time of my

~Have a Magical Day~

life. I was so depressed that I quit my job, spent all my money, and maxed out all my credit cards shopping and indulging in food. I lost everything. I lost my best friend and biggest supporter. I lost my savings. And I lost my passion for life.

I spent months sulking and having self-pity and woe is my party. Then I realized something. Life is too short to live depressed. Life is too short to not enjoy every single day. So instead of making a list in my mind about all the reasons why this was a terrible thing, I decided to do what my mom taught me to do, which was to count my blessings. I then recited and made a gratitude list of why this was a beautiful thing.

~Have a Magical Day~

I'm thankful that she's no longer in pain. I'm thankful that I don't have to see her suffer. I'm thankful that I can now spend more time with my family and develop a closer relationship with my dad, which I didn't have before. I'm thankful that I can now devote my time and energy to using this situation to fuel my goals and dreams and not destroy them. I'm thankful that this trying time has made me stronger.

I did this exercise day in and day out, and shortly afterwards, things began to magically change in my life. At the time, I was jobless and living in freezing cold, NJ. I landed a new job in sunny beautiful San Diego, California. I regained my health and had way more energy. I started my own consulting business called Hope

~Have a Magical Day~

Nuggets, which has reached millions of people worldwide. In addition, I regained my passion for life! Gratitude changed me! And it can change you!

You now know that you can take any negative situation and turn it into something beautiful simply by looking for things to be grateful for about the situation. This is how I live my life every single day. Gratitude is not just a daily practice in the morning, it's a lifestyle. It's a lifestyle of being happy. It's a way of life that will bring you so much magic!

A lot of people tell me I will be happy when my kids go to college. I will be happy when I get the promotion. I will be happy when I get a new house. I'll definitely be happy when I finally get married.

~Have a Magical Day~

We currently live in such a fast-paced society. Everyone wants the new iPhone when the one you have still works. We want to sleep with it before we put a ring on it. We want the promotion, but we show up late to the job we currently have. Those aspiring homeowners can't even clean their tiny apartment. Also, if you're not happy before you meet the man or woman of your dreams, you certainly won't find lasting happiness when you meet them! You have to be happy with yourself first before you can be happy with someone else!

Part of this gratitude way of life is finding a way to be content. Being content means that you're happy with where you are while still pursuing your dreams! Being content means you're not trying to rush God's timing but

~Have a Magical Day~

that you'll keep doing and being your best while waiting on His promises! Contentment is such a beautiful thing. You no longer depend on people and circumstances to make you happy.

I know you want that management position, but are you ready to handle and manage different personalities? I know that dream home is within reach, but are you prepared for the responsibility of maintaining a bigger house? I know you're praying for that wedding ring, but are you sure you're ready? Are you prepared to deal with occasional drama?

I'm not saying to stop pursuing these things. I encourage you to pursue your dreams daily with renewed vigor. Just make sure you're grateful and happy with where you currently are at this moment. This prevents you from depending on accomplishments to make you happy. This keeps you humble. If you're not happy with where you are now, you'll never get to where you want to be.

Be grateful for the job you have now. Be grateful for the car and the money and the health you have right now. Give thanks for all the amazing relationships you have right now.

I've discovered that in your life, something will always be dying while something else is being born.

For all those out there struggling with depression and anxiety, let me share these hope nuggets with you. I mentioned this earlier, and I will reiterate. It is a scientifically proven fact that you cannot feel grateful and

~Have a Magical Day~

sad at the same time. It is literally impossible! The beautiful thing about this is that you have the power to decide what you want to feel here by choosing what you focus on.

So many people wake up and feel depressed because they first think depressing thoughts. They think depressing memories. Let me ask you, what are you focusing on?

We have the power to choose what we focus on! A bad memory can't make you feel bad anymore today. It already happened! It can only continue to make you feel sad if you continue to dwell on it.

Want to know something powerful I've learned? When you walk in faith, sometimes you can't make the fear and anxiety go away. However, it doesn't have to be in your frame! You can be in the midst of fear, but it doesn't have to get in your system. You don't have to ask God to give you more faith and gratitude. Faith and gratitude are all a matter of focus.

Just as starting your day with gratitude is important, it's just as important to end your day with gratitude as well. I'll tell you why.

I would say about 95 percent of the human population wakes up grumpy and goes to bed anxious. We already know now that waking up and starting your day in a bad mood starts a cycle of unpleasant events in your day.

~Have a Magical Day~

Have you ever considered that maybe you woke up grumpy because you went to bed anxious? Going to bed feeling anxiety, depression, and discouragement will lead to a vicious cycle of starting the following day on the wrong side of the bed.

To combat this, you have to develop the habit of going to bed grateful! I learned in the book 'The Magic' by Rhonda Byrne that you should keep what's called a 'Magic Gratitude Rock.'

You can get yourself any rock at any place you want as long as it can fit comfortably in your hand. Before I go to bed every night, I hold my magic gratitude rock in my hand and give God thanks for everything that went well in my day.

~Have a Magical Day~

I'm grateful for all the food I ate. I'm grateful for the amazing workout I had. I'm appreciative of the catch-up date I had with one of my best friends. I give thanks for the fact that I was divinely protected and didn't get into any accidents. I'm grateful for the sunrise and sunset. I'm grateful for my tired body because it means I was able to work hard.

The list doesn't have to be crazy long as long as you feel the feelings of gratitude as you recall these events. After you make your list, you then want to give thanks for the thing you are MOST grateful for. Give God praise for the BEST thing that happened to you that day.

~Have a Magical Day~

This exercise completely obliterates feelings of anxiety and worry and creates a momentum of joy and gratitude for the next day, which will lead to more magic!

It's incredibly easy for us to focus on our failures instead of being grateful for our victories. It's not hard to focus on how far we have to go as opposed to being grateful for how far we have come. But again, you have that choice! Choose gratitude for all the good in your life!

Make a concerted effort to ditch the complaints and make gratitude a way of life! Get in the habit of reciting, verbalizing, and really feeling the feelings of gratitude for all your blessings daily, and I promise you your days will be filled with Magic!

2

Chapter 2: Be a Blessing

'You can have whatever you want in life if you can help enough people get what they want.' – Zig Ziglar-

We live in a society where the motto is to look out for number one. What's in it for me? We have the mentality that says, 'I can help you, but how does this benefit me?'

When we live with a 'me me me' mentality, we won't live to our fullest potential. However, when you give what you have, when you desire to be a blessing, you will never go

without it! A closed hand cannot give or receive blessings.

~Have a Magical Day~

'You have not lived today until you have done something for someone who cannot repay you.'

–Jon Bunyan-

One of the most significant revelations and epiphanies I've ever had was that every day we should reach what I like to call the 'Blessing Quota.' For those who work in sales, you know all about reaching quotas and sales goals in order to get compensated.

The 'Blessing Quota' is a little bit different. With this quota, your objective is to find at least one person that you can bless, at least one person that you can inspire or make smile. You should aim to do at least one random act of kindness per day.

~Have a Magical Day~

It doesn't have to be anything big. It can be as little as opening a door for a handicapped person or giving a hug to someone who looks like they need it. You can buy your coworker lunch when he or she forgot their wallet at home.

I promise that when you do this, your levels of happiness will increase dramatically. When you look to be a blessing, blessings will start looking for you.

A random act of kindness per day can do wonders. It can boost happiness, lower blood pressure, decrease stress, release feel-good chemicals, and inspire more kindness!

Luke 6:38 in the Bible says, 'Give, and it shall be given unto you; good measure, pressed down, and shaken together, and running over, shall men give into your bosom.'

Like I stated in chapter one, it doesn't matter whether you're religious or not. It doesn't matter if you call it 'karma,' 'sowing and reaping,' or 'vibrations and energy.' What you give will always be given unto you. The energy you give out is the energy that will return to you, good or bad.

If you smile at people, people will smile back at you. If you open doors for people, doors will surely be opened for you. When you love others, God will make sure that you are loved as well.

I heard a story about a woman who was diagnosed with terminal cancer. She was told by her doctors that she

~Have a Magical Day~

only had a few months to live. She, along with her entire family, was devastated by the news. At this very moment, she had a decision to make. She had the choice to make between feeling sorry for herself and taking actions toward the miraculous.

She made the conscious decision to visit her local hospital and pray for hundreds of sick people. She laid hands and declared complete healing over every sick person she came in contact with. This woman stopped focusing on herself. She rid herself of any form of selfishness and displayed an amazing sense of courage and selflessness. Giving up and wallowing in self-pity was the easier choice. Not for this brave soul. She chose to be a blessing.

~Have a Magical Day~

A few months later, she gained back the weight she lost when she was diagnosed. Her body began to function the way it's supposed to. She got better and better each passing day. A few more weeks later, the doctors that told her she was going to die were utterly shocked that she was miraculously healed!

Instead of being buried, she buried her sickness. She buried any form of selfishness and truly experienced the power of being a blessing to others. If you're sick today, be like this woman and pray for those who are sick. If you're lonely, befriend others who are lonely.

If you own a company and business is slow, help other businesses grow. If you're single and looking for your soul mate, help your fellow single friend find the

~Have a Magical Day~

love of their life. Don't be surprised if yours walks right into your life!

In 1995, preemie twins Brielle and Kyrie Jackson were born. They were 12 weeks premature, and the nurses concluded that one of the babies was not expected to live. One of the hospital nurses fought through hoops and bounds to get the twins in the same incubator.

She successfully got them in the same incubator, and the stronger baby put her arm around her sister, who wasn't expected to make it. Her touch allowed the struggling baby's heart to stabilize along with her temperature returning to normal. In due time, both twins made it and left that hospital completely healthy! Today they are known as the "Rescuing Hug" twins.

~Have a Magical Day~

My friends, somebody needs your touch. Somebody needs your smile, your presence, your love. Life isn't all about you. It's about being a blessing to others.

Who can you bless today? Who can you hug? Who can you help heal? Whose life can you turn around?

I heard Will Smith saying that when you make other people's lives better, your life will automatically be better as a result.

In this world, there are takers and givers.

Takers love to receive and take way more from others than they give. They specialize in taking credit for things and occasional backstabbing. Takers love to keep knowledge for themselves and not share their wisdom with the world.

I've met many successful business owners who absolutely refused to share how they became successful. They have the mentality that if they share their knowledge, they will lose. They're so wrong. These are the types of people that end up unhappy and unfulfilled, no matter how much success they accumulate.

On the other hand, givers actually enjoy sharing their wisdom and knowledge. They like contributing more to people than they receive in return and offer help without expecting anything in return and with no strings attached.

~Have a Magical Day~

Givers are winners. Givers are happy. Givers succeed in their careers, in their health, in their finances, and in their relationships.

There are many benefits to being generous. Generosity actually promotes physical health. Physical and mental health improves after just one act of kindness.

Giving improves blood pressure the same way exercise and medicine do.

Being a generous giver encourages and leads to personal happiness. Some of us don't know our purpose here on earth. I believe we're here to love, be loved, and give. When you freely give your time, resources, and energy, it gives you a renewed sense of purpose and naturally fights depression and anxiety.

~Have a Magical Day~

Giving flat out feels good. You give off the emotion of happiness, and in return, you will receive more things that will make you happy.

Making an effort to be a giver will also reduce stress. Did you know that being selfish and stingy is connected to higher levels of cortisol? Cortisol is your body's stress hormone. The more you give, the less stressed you are.

I firmly believe in eating healthy and working out regularly to live a long and satisfying life. However, it has been proven time and time again that generosity will increase your lifespan!

~Have a Magical Day~

I heard that the University of Buffalo discovered that being unselfish decreased your chances of experiencing an early death.

Giving also helps you in all of your relationships. It will help build your marriage, strengthen your relationships with family and friends, and build deeper connections with your co-workers.

Can you imagine a world where everyone made an effort to give? There would be so much love and gratitude. There would be no room for anxiety or depression because everyone would be rooting for each other to succeed instead of being in competition. There would be less jealousy, strife, hate, and bitterness.

~Have a Magical Day~

Would you like to increase your financial health? Give! Find a nonprofit organization that you believe in and support them financially.

If your friend mentions that they won't have money until payday and you invite them out to eat, grab their tab this time.

When you give, you can't help but receive more blessings in return when you give with the right attitude.

When you give to get, that defeats the purpose. That means you're thinking about yourself. However, when you give knowing that you may or may not get anything back, that's when those blessings flow.

Another important note that can't be ignored is you have to make sure you don't become an irresponsible giver. Yes, you read that right. It's very possible to give irresponsibly.

In my earlier years, I would find five nonprofit organizations to support. I would lend money to every single friend who was struggling. I gave to every cause and always gave my time and energy even though I knew I needed rest.

I want you to know that it's amazing to be a giver, but you can't help everybody. You can't keep giving but not have any leftover for yourself. You can't take care of others if you don't first take care of yourself.

Similarly, don't help people who don't help themselves. If you give resources to someone who isn't

~Have a Magical Day~

trying to get resources on their own, then you're just enabling them and becoming a crutch for them.

It's one thing to help someone who's stuck on the side of the freeway when their car breaks down. It's another thing to help someone who's pushing their car and making an effort to fix it. People love to help others who are already helping themselves.

So be a giver, but a responsible one.

One thing you should always give to the world is your talent. If you have been blessed with gifts and talents, it would be an absolute crime if you didn't share it with everyone. If you can sing, let the world hear your voice. If you can cook, share that gift. If you can speak in public, let that talent develop so you can change lives.

~Have a Magical Day~

Remember, we're not blessed just so we can receive blessings and enjoy them for ourselves. We're blessed so we can be a blessing!

If you're experiencing more than your share of problems right now, turn things around by helping others with their problems. The world would be a much better and happier place if we all lifted each other up!

~Have a Magical Day~

3

Chapter 3: Visualize your Success

'When you visualize, then you materialize.'

– Denis Waitley-

The word visualize means to form a mental image of or to imagine. Most people don't realize it, but they form mental images of things they don't want. They unintentionally visualize having bad days and then wonder why problems occur as they leave their house. They visualize being stuck in traffic. They form a picture in their minds of the sales day being slow. Or receiving bad news.

~Have a Magical Day~

What I've learned is that you decide what you visualize! You hold the power to imagine anything. So why not imagine what you want? When you hold a picture in your mind and believe it long enough, it manifests!

If you think down, you will go down. If you think up, you will go up. You'll always travel in the direction of your thinking.

T. D. Jakes

Why not visualize your day being amazing? Why not visualize passing that exam in flying colors? Why don't you imagine closing deals at work easily and effortlessly?

"Whatever your mind can conceive and believe, it can achieve." –Napoleon Hill-

~Have a Magical Day~

Before you leave your house, after you have finished the gratitude practice outlined in chapter one, and after you have made the decision to find at least one person you can bless, you can now move on to visualizing a magical day.

"Imagination is everything. It is the preview of life's coming attractions." – Albert Einstein-

Remember when we were kids, we would always play? I learned and discovered that the greatest playground and the greatest nation is our imagination. However, too many of us have let the circumstances of life ruin God's most excellent playground for us.

Your mind and imagination are where you're supposed to hold your greatest visions and dreams, not your fears. Your mind is where you're supposed to hold the Promises of God, not the lies of the enemy.

I want you to right now serve an eviction notice. You need to serve an eviction notice to your fears; an eviction notice needs to be sent to your anxiety and worry. Now it's time to welcome in love, joy, peace, gratitude, happiness, and kindness. When you make this decision, your life will never be the same. Let's play!

"Visualization is daydreaming with a purpose."

– Bo Bennett-

Did you know that every single invention and accomplishment started in someone's imagination? The Wright brothers imagined flying in a piece of metal before their vision of the airplane manifested.

~Have a Magical Day~

The smartphone you use daily was first just an idea. Every single appliance in your home started to come to fruition when someone imagined it and took action.

You hold this same power to envision amazing days and amazing accomplishments.

When you decide to visualize, don't let this become a chore. Have fun with it! To start with, sit alone and relax your body. Meditate and say to yourself that the forces that are working for you are greater than the forces against you. This puts you in a state of confidence that this will work.

Then visualize your day in great detail. Be very specific. Set in your mind a clear and detailed mental image of what you desire to accomplish that day. Imagine that meeting going well. If you're a parent, imagine your children behaving and having great days at school. If you have an office job, imagine getting things done on time.

Imagine everything on your to-do list getting done without missing a single item.

If you work in retail, visualize happy customers coming your way instead of grumpy ones. Put feelings and emotions into what you are visualizing. Then finally, entertain only positive thoughts, feelings, and words.

When you first start visualizing, it might be a little tricky. Your mind may automatically start thinking negative. You might feel feelings of worry and anxiety over your to-do list. That's completely normal! We all feel overwhelmed at times. All of these methods are new

~Have a Magical Day~

ways of thinking and being. It's definitely going to take time and practice to master visualizing success, especially if you've spent the majority of your life worried and stressed over how things will work out in your life.

One of the most powerful things you can do to master the art of visualizing is by creating your own vision board. It doesn't have to be anything fancy. You can buy a regular piece of cardboard at the dollar store and use it as your vision board. Then you want to print out pictures of your desires and paste them on the board. Print out a photo of the house you want, the car you want, the ring that you want to buy for your future spouse, or anything that your heart truly desires.

~Have a Magical Day~

Afterwards, go ahead and spend a few minutes looking intently at your board and feel the feelings of gratitude as if you already have those desires. Close your eyes and use your imagination to visualize receiving them. Feel the joy. Feel the love. Feel the excitement. Do this at least twice a day, and you will attract and manifest those wishes.

Visualizing daily has many benefits. One of them is stress relief! Visualization is a form of relaxation which naturally decreases stress.

Your happiness levels will increase when you visualize. When you imagine having something you really want, your levels of joy increase.

~Have a Magical Day~

Yes, you may not be in a position to have it just yet. Always remember that your mind doesn't know the difference between what's real or make-believe during the act of visualizing. This brings you one step closer to literally having your desires.

When you relax and quiet your mind to visualize, you are actually improving your ability to focus. You won't be bound by limitations and restrictions. With practice, you will get better, and your focus will be immaculate.

For those who are sick, you can visualize yourself to better health. Have you noticed that when you have an unusual cough or symptom, you google it, and then you read about all these other diseases and symptoms, and then you start to feel them. What just happened? You created sickness in your body by unintentionally visualizing that you were sick and had those symptoms.

If you can create sickness with your mind, then you can create amazing health as well! Imagine having perfect health. Imagine having amazing youth, energy, and vitality! Visualize yourself achieving your perfect weight.

Make-believe you already have the body you want.

Let me share a story about how powerful this is. Back in 2012, I got hired at Bank of America as a personal banker. It was a great job, and I truly excelled at it. After a few years, I decided that I wanted to become a small business banker because I was passionate about helping businesses grow along with the fact that it was going to be a significant increase in pay. I took my business card that said 'personal banker' and crossed out my job title. I wrote on the business card the position I wanted, which was 'small business banker.' I pasted this altered business card on my vision board, and I looked at it every day before I left my house and every night before I went to sleep. I would visualize in great detail having that new job.

I visualized my new desk. I imagined taking business clients out to lunch. I imagined receiving my paycheck with a higher pay rate. I pictured in my mind leading my team in sales. I visualized how much fun I was

~Have a Magical Day~

having in my new position. It became so real in my mind that it brought tears to my eyes. When you start crying during a visualization session, you've reached a high level of spiritual energy that will cause a quick manifestation.

I did this exercise every single day. I did not go a day without imagining that new job. A few months later, I got the position! When I got hired, it didn't surprise me because I had already been there in my mind so many times. Not only did I get the job, but I became the number one small business banker in my market!

Pastor Marcus Gill once said, "You have to see it before you see it, or you never will see it."

That's more than worth repeating.

~Have a Magical Day~

"You have to see it before you see it, or you never will see it."

In other words, you have to see it in your mind, or you will never ever hold it in your hand.

I currently reside in San Diego, California. My younger sister and I grew up in a small town, Bergenfield, New Jersey. I moved to San Diego in 2012. Every time my sister would visit, she would fall in love with the city. She fell in love with the sunshine, the palm trees, and the amazing weather year-round. She had a very strong desire for her and her husband to move here. However, they had no idea how it would happen.

Too many people experience doubts about their dreams coming to life because they focus on how they

~Have a Magical Day~

will get there. Your job is not to figure out how. Your job is to believe. God will take care of the 'how.'

My sister did what I'm asking you to do. She visualized moving to California. She took gorgeous photos of the city and placed them where she can look at them every single day. She imagined what it would be like to live in Cali and not have to deal with cold weather anymore.

There were definitely moments of doubt. She would often call me and tell me she had no idea how she would get a job across the country and how she would be able to afford it. I told her to hold on to the dream and keep visualizing every single day and not to quit in moments of doubt.

~Have a Magical Day~

Full disclaimer – the doubts will come. Fears and negative thoughts will come. However, you need to have faith. Faith isn't the absence of doubt; it's the ability to push through the doubts and enter your destiny.

After a few months, her dream manifested. In a wild and crazy sequence of events, she interviewed with an amazing company and landed her dream job in San Diego!

Once again, forget about the 'how.'

The 'how' is what causes people to doubt and give up. Most successful people understand that 'how' isn't important. They don't care about how or when they'll get to their destination. They just believe in their

~Have a Magical Day~

heart of hearts with unwavering faith that they will get there.

Back in 2010, one of my favorite athletes of all time, Kobe Bryant found himself in the NBA finals against the Boston Celtics.

After the series was over, a reporter asked Kobe if he ever doubted that his team would win. He said that he knew his team would find a way to win. However, he just didn't know 'how.'

Even the great ones understand that the 'how' part of your vision coming to life is unimportant. God has so many ways to provide.

The universe has a million and a half ways to get you to your dream. We're not called to understand how.

~Have a Magical Day~

We're called to follow God through the process of life's journey.

Believe me when I say this works! It will not happen overnight. There will be times when you think you're wasting your time. That's when you need to dig your heels in and truly believe that what you're visualizing will happen! Again, when you hold on to a vision in your mind long enough and truly believe it with every fiber of your being, you will eventually experience a divine manifestation.

4

Chapter 4: Forgive Others

When someone does you wrong, one of the easiest things to do is hold a grudge. As a matter of fact, it's the natural thing to do. It's human nature to be upset. However, one of the unhealthiest things you can do is begin to harbor unforgiveness in your heart. Life is too short for that. Life is too short to live unhappy because of a person or event.

Holding on to the pain of what someone said about you or did to you is actually bad for your health. Your immune system literally gets weaker when you don't forgive. You may experience tension in your neck

~Have a Magical Day~

and shoulders, and you may even feel pain in your bones.

You can also start to lose hair due to stress.

You can't have a magical day if you're holding on to the hurts of yesterday. You can't be truly happy if you have bitterness towards another person. There's so much power in letting go. There's so much pain involved in holding on.

I hear you saying, "Wendell, they never apologized to me!"

Sometimes you have to be strong enough to forgive without receiving an apology. Let go, even though you never got the 'I'm sorry' you were hoping for. It will be so liberating and freeing.

~Have a Magical Day~

You have to be bigger than what happened to you. It's your birthright to be free, so stop giving that right over to someone else. When the thought of what someone did to you in the past triggers you, then you've given that person or situation all the power. You need to take your passion, power, and joy back. It all starts with letting go.

I believe that anxiety is at an all-time high in our society these days. So many people are not living in peace. Part of it is because of not being able to let go of the past.

You have to sow a seed of forgiveness so that you can receive a harvest of peace. You have to let go of yesterday's hurts so you can experience the magic of today and abundance in your future.

~Have a Magical Day~

Don't carry yesterday's baggage into the gift of today. That co-worker that got on your nerves yesterday, that argument you got into with your spouse last night, or that negative comment you received on social media; Let it go. Dwelling on these things drain your energy. They rob you of your joy and creativity.

You won't have the strength to fight today's battles when you're still battling with the events of yesterday.

Whenever you're feeling triggered by a negative event that happened or by what someone did to you, here's my recommendation – and I know this isn't easy, especially when the person hurt you. However, try to send love and good vibes their way. Wish them well. When you give love, you receive love. When you give out feelings of anger and bitterness, you will experience events today that will cause you to continue feeling anger and bitterness.

Our vibrations and emotions are boomerangs and echoes. Whatever you give out comes right back to you.

There are so many benefits to practicing forgiveness. Forgiving will lead to healthier relationships. Your heart health will improve. You may notice lower blood pressure. Anxiety, stress, and hostility will dissipate. Both your mental health and immune system will improve.

Any symptoms of depression will also die down when you forgive.

~Have a Magical Day~

Here's how you know you've fully forgiven someone; when you don't feel triggered by them anymore. You know you've moved on when the mere thought of them no longer makes your blood boil and when you're able to have an adult conversation with them.

However, here's a caveat that I want everyone to fully grasp and comprehend. If someone who you thought was your friend did you wrong, yes, you forgive them. Yes, you let go and move on. Then again, this doesn't mean you have to remain friends with them.

Some people think they have to stay close to the people who hurt them. That's not the case. When someone hurts you and shows you signs that this is who they are and what they're capable of continuing to do, you are not

~Have a Magical Day~

obligated to stay friends after forgiving them. Otherwise, you're just opening the door to more pain in the future.

Forgive, wish them well, send love, and then move on with your life. It's okay to love people from a distance.

This is especially true when it comes to family and relatives. Don't get me wrong, I'm all about family, and I believe in keeping family close. However, if an aunt, uncle, cousin, brother, or sister displays toxic behavior and does you wrong and displays the potential to do you wrong again in the future, you have to distance yourself. Toxic is toxic, no matter who it is.

Keep the people close to you who inspire you and bring out the best in you, not those who drain your energy.

~Have a Magical Day~

We all need people cheering us on. We need people who celebrate us and genuinely wish us well, even if it means that we do better than them or have more success than them. These are the people you need to stay close to.

So again, if anyone did you wrong or if any events from yesterday really disturbed you, let go and move on, and make the conscious decision on who to keep and remove from your life.

When you forgive, you're not doing it for the other person. You're doing it for you. You're doing it for your sanity, for your peace of mind, for your health.

I once heard Lewis B. Smedes say, "To forgive is to set a prisoner free and discover that the prisoner was you."

5

Chapter 5: Love Yourself

Every single morning, you ought to wake up, look in the mirror, and say 'Good morning, beautiful! It's gonna be a great day. I give you permission to prosper. You are worthy to receive all forms of magnificence. And anybody would be lucky to have you!'

I've learned another thing. I learned that one of the best types of love is self-love.

I'm not talking about being conceited. I'm talking about healthy self-respect for you. If you don't have respect for yourself, the world won't respect you. If you don't love you, no one else can truly and fully love you.

~Have a Magical Day~

Appreciate the beauty that God has put on the inside of you. When you fall in love with you, the whole world will fall in love with you too.

Too many people place their self-worth in other people's hands. There are millions of people who live off of other's compliments and validation. My nugget for you regarding this is that you are not a parking ticket. You don't need to be validated by others. The fact that the Creator of the Universe values you and loves you more than you can imagine is enough validation and enough cause to feel good about yourself.

For all the single people out there, when you learn to truly love yourself, that's when you're the most attractive. When you have low self-esteem, you give off a

~Have a Magical Day~

needy and desperate vibe, and you scare away any potential suitors.

"The funny thing is when you start feeling happy alone, that's when everyone decides to be with you" – Jim Carrey -

So many people think that they need to find someone to complete them. If you need someone to complete you, you are going to enter a destined to fail relationship because that is too much pressure to put on another person. No one can truly complete you except you. You need to find completeness and wholeness as an individual before meeting your soul mate.

~Have a Magical Day~

When two halves come together, it's a disaster. But when two happy and whole people come together, that's magical.

If you don't love yourself, you can't expect others to love you either. Loving yourself also means taking care of yourself, physically and mentally.

From a physical standpoint, you have to take care of your body. Get enough sleep every night. Drink enough water. Exercise at least three times per week. Avoid processed foods and foods that are high in sugar. You can't be your absolute best when you're feeling sluggish and lethargic. You won't have magical days when you depend on 4 cups of coffee to keep you awake. All that will do is lead to incredible crashes and tons of anxious nights.

A lot of people don't love themselves because they're not happy with the way they look or because they are not satisfied with certain physical features.

I often hear things like, "I wish I were taller."

"I wish I was a different race."

If God wanted you to be taller, He would have made you taller. Be proud of your ethnicity! God made you that height and ethnicity for a reason, and you should fully embrace it. Learn to love every single physical feature you have. Love your eyes, your nose, your lips, your face, your hair, your hips, your curves, and your body type. You are made in the image of God, and He doesn't make mistakes! You are beautiful and perfect just as you are!

Another way to truly love and take care of yourself is to maximize your alone time. It's very easy to not realize that people can absolutely drain your energy. There are a lot of individuals out there who are energy-sucking vampires. When you don't take time to be alone and recharge, you will burn out.

During this alone time, I highly recommend meditation, yoga, going to the gym, doing a hike outdoors, watching the sunrise and sunset, seeing your favorite movie, getting a massage, doing a cryotherapy or float session, visiting a chiropractor, etc. There are so many things you can do alone that will revitalize you. Take

~Have a Magical Day~

advantage of this time. Do what you love and what brings you joy.

People often tell me that they don't have time. When you truly love yourself, you prioritize your wellbeing and make time for yourself.

I learned a very powerful phrase, and I'm so excited to share it with you.

That powerful phrase is just one word and one syllable. It starts with an N and ends with an O.

"No."

You have to learn when to say no. A huge reason why people are so anxious is that they say yes to every event, yes to every gathering, yes to every function that they know they don't have the energy for.

~Have a Magical Day~

Saying no in order to take care of yourself is one of the most profound and freeing things you can do. Nothing will suck your energy quite like having too many commitments that you cannot stick to.

So let's practice saying this out loud together.

"No."

That had to have felt good!

Get in the habit of saying 'no' to things you don't have the energy for. At the same time, make sure that when you do commit, you honor your word.

I want you all to understand that you are valuable. I want you to know your true worth. You are amazing. You are magnificent. There is no one else on this earth like you. You are one of a kind.

~Have a Magical Day~

When you realize your value, and how special you are, you will walk around with newfound confidence. Having confidence and self-love has so many benefits.

Being confident leads to more happiness and joy in your life. The more self-confident you are, the happier you are with yourself, and you naturally enjoy more of what life has to offer.

When you are confident, people notice and are gravitated towards you. You attract blessings by default when you are full of self-love and confidence.

Having confidence and self-love means that you are on a high vibration. This energy is contagious and magnetic. This type of energy leads to happiness and peace.

~Have a Magical Day~

However, you have to do your job to protect this peace and energy. Universal forces will try to rob you of this peace.

To protect your peace, you need to distance yourself from toxic people. There's nothing quite as energy-draining as being around someone who is negative and full of complaints and sorrow. Their lack of positive energy has the ability to drain you of all the positive energy that you worked so hard to obtain.

Being surrounded by people who constantly complain can be detrimental to your health.

Next time when you're around someone who is complaining and has bad energy, find a way to politely excuse yourself. I promise you it's worth doing.

~Have a Magical Day~

It's better than staying in that room and engaging in that energy-draining conversation.

To protect your valuable energy, it's okay to say no. It's okay to cancel a commitment. It's perfectly fine to take a day off and do nothing. It's a beautiful thing to want to be alone. It's normal and justifiable to not want to answer that phone call.

As you implement these self-love and self-care techniques, you won't be drained and in need of a nap by 2pm. For all my introverts out there, you won't need to be carried off on a stretcher after attending that social event. You will have a healthy sustained peace and energy.

~Have a Magical Day~

As you learn to love you and take care of you, you'll soon fall in love with you. That's when the rest of the world will fall in love with you too.

6

Chapter 6: Speak it into your Existence

"Death and Life are in the Power of the tongue..."

Proverbs 18:21

Besides watching your own thoughts and feelings, another thing to be completely mindful and conscious of are the words that come out of your mouth. Words are like seeds, and when you say something long enough, your subconscious mind believes it and starts acting as if it's true.

~Have a Magical Day~

One of the most powerful phrases in the world is "I Am." It's incredibly powerful because what follows the "I Am" follows you.

If you walk around saying, "I Am Blessed," blessings follow you. What follows "I am healthy" is life and vitality. Following your declaration of "I am successful" is a tremendous amount of success.

This works in reverse as well. When you say "I am broke," poverty will follow you. When you say, "I am unhappy," then sadness will follow you. When you say "I am fat," calories and slow metabolism will follow you. Saying the phrase "I am always sick" will be followed by bad health.

~Have a Magical Day~

I fully believe in saying affirmations every morning. You have the power to literally attract what you're affirming when you say them with full faith and belief that they're true. Sometimes when you say affirmations, at first, it will feel like a lie. It may feel awkward and uncomfortable. But keep saying them.

The more you say them, the more your subconscious mind will believe it. Let me share with you some of the affirmations I say that have brought a tremendous amount of happiness and success.

"I am beautiful."

"I am talented."

"I am strong."

"I am healthy."

~Have a Magical Day~

"I am harmonious and happy."

"Good things always happen to me."

"I'm very lucky when it comes to money."

"I'm a winner. I'm a champion."

"Everything always seems to work out for me."

"People love me and love being around me."

"I have the perfect body."

Again, some of these may feel like a lie at first. Shake off those funny feelings and keep saying them daily. You will eventually get to the point where you actually believe them, and you will give life to these affirmations, and they will literally manifest before your very eyes.

~Have a Magical Day~

Did you know that with your words, you can either bless your future or curse it? The choice is yours.

I see too many people going around saying things like, "I'm always sick and tired."

"Nothing good ever happens to me."

"Nobody's attracted to me, and I can't find a date."

"I'm so fat."

And then they wonder why things won't change. Start adding those affirmations that I previously stated and watch things turn around.

Scripture says that you need to call the things that are not as though they already are. That means you have to speak health before you see it. You need to declare that

~Have a Magical Day~

you're blessed before you actually start seeing blessings.

You have to declare that you're prosperous before the

prosperity and wealth show up.

Before you leave the house or before you leave

your car and walk into work, start declaring, and "Today

is going to be a great day. Today, my family and I are

going to be blessed. Today, we're going to be a blessing.

Today, we're going to accomplish our goals."

As you do this daily and believe it with all your

heart, watch the magic happen!

~Have a Magical Day~

7

Chapter 7: Dance like You Already Got It

"Therefore I tell you, whatever you ask for in prayer, believe that you have received it, and it will be yours." ~Mark 11:24~

Jesus literally tells us to believe we already received what we asked for. If your prayer request got answered today, how would you respond? Some would shout. Some would jump for joy. Some would post it on social media so all their friends could see.

~Have a Magical Day~

You know what I would do? I would dance. It's one of the greatest forms of celebration. The point is, you're going to give off amazing vibes if your dream comes true. You would be incredibly happy if you got the job, closed the sale, passed the test, received the brand new car, etc.

To receive, you have to believe you've already received it. You need to speak, think, act, and live your life as if it's already done. You need to live in the end result.

Allow me to share with you one of the most powerful practices that I've done over the last few years that has changed my life dramatically. This practice has helped me achieve great success in my career, amazing

~Have a Magical Day~

health, financial abundance, perfect peace, indescribable joy, and the opportunity to be happy every single day no matter what is happening around me. This has brought me so much joy, and it has defined my purpose.

After I do my morning prayer, which is usually in my car, I play one of my favorite songs, and I dance in my car. However, I don't dance in vain. I dance as if the day ahead was already magical. I dance to celebrate what God has already done in my life. I dance with gratitude for all that I have right now. And I dance with amazing joy and energy as if what I'm desiring has already happened.

When Jesus told us to believe that we have received it that means we need to feel the feelings of having it now. This is the fastest way to manifest your desires and set the tone to have an amazing day. What

better way to feel the feelings of having it now than by

dancing?

The car dance is powerful because you will

automatically give off good vibrations. Remember, I

mentioned earlier that the vibe you give out is what

determines what you receive. Playing your favorite song

will immediately make you at least ten percent happier

and shift your mood and then adding your dance moves

and visualizations allow you to be in a different

stratosphere. When you do this properly, your

imagination will run wild, and it will feel so real. When

you get to the point where what's make-believe in your

~Have a Magical Day~

mind feels so real, that's what sets the miracle in motion for you to receive it.

You'll be in a stratosphere of love, positivity, faith, and expectation. It will be very difficult to have a bad day after doing the morning car dance.

Back in 2017, I worked in sales for this large corporation. I had a goal to be the absolute best at what I did. Every morning, I would do the morning dance routine and dance as if I had an amazing sales day. I bopped to the music as if clients said yes, and that deals were closed left and right. I didn't miss a single day. I did the car dance in the morning, and I never let it get boring. I always found a way to have fun with it.

~Have a Magical Day~

That year I finished in the top one percent in sales for that company, and I won a free trip to Miami with a stay at a 5-star hotel.

So many people tell me, "I'll dance when I get my desire. I'll dance when the promotion comes. I'll dance when my prayers get answered."

You've got it backwards, the dance comes first. The celebration in your heart and mind must take place first in order to speed up your manifestation.

I heard about this American Indian tribe that was known for their rain dances. Whenever a city was in a drought, they would call on this particular tribe to dance. Without fail, every time they danced, it would rain.

~Have a Magical Day~

A community leader asked the head chief, 'Hey! How come every time you dance it rains?'

The chief said, 'It's very simple. We dance until it rains.'

My encouragement to you is that you pray until it rains. Praise God, believe, and live with expectations until your dreams happen. Then they will happen!

So dance like you got it and dance till you get it!

Then you have to go into your day walking around like you already have it.

If your dream is to have a million-dollar business, and that dream had already come true, would you walk around with your shoulders slouched?

Absolutely not!

~Have a Magical Day~

You would walk around with amazing posture, and you'd be sticking out your chest. Walk around like that now! Feel that vibration of abundance now!

One of my closest friends had a dream to have a baby girl. She already had two boys who were in their teens. Being a mom had become her life purpose, and she loved every moment of it. She raised her two boys to be amazing men. Nevertheless, she still wanted a baby girl. She wanted her own princess, who would grow up to be a magnificent queen.

The doctors told her she was at high risk. Her own thoughts told her it wasn't going to happen. She tried for years and failed. There were more than a few moments where she wanted to give up and settle.

~Have a Magical Day~

However, I told her God put that dream in her heart for a reason. Then, I let her know that she needed to take action. So she did what I'm asking you to do when it comes to your most important goals and dreams.

You need to visualize it happening in your mind. You then need to declare positive words proclaiming that it will happen. And then you gotta dance like it already happened.

Every morning she did this exercise. She didn't do it as a mundane routine. She had fun with it. She made preparations for her dream to come to pass. Soon enough, she got the news that she was pregnant with a baby girl. Her dream came true and manifested!

~Have a Magical Day~

Often times, after you do the car dance, events may occur during the day that are the complete opposite of what you just finished dancing to. Don't let that discourage you. These are just tests of faith. God will often send tests to see how bad you really want it. You can't just kind of want it.

Psalm 37:4 says that God will give you your heart's desires, but you have to desire them with all your heart. Part of showing God how bad you want it is visualizing and dancing, even when you don't see it yet. This is what faith is all about. Believing in something you don't see just yet. However, the reward of this faith is seeing these visions come to life.

~Have a Magical Day~

So when you dance as if you had an amazing day and the day didn't go quite as amazing, don't stop doing the car dance. God causes everything to work for you and causes everything to benefit you. That means both good days and bad days will help you grow.

However, doing the car dance and the previous steps outlined in this book ensures that you always win in the end. When I won that award for being a top seller, I didn't have a great sales day every single day.

There were some days where I got no sales at all. However, that didn't stop me from dancing in my car like a crazy person every morning. I had unwavering faith that I would come out on top in the end. When you do this,

~Have a Magical Day~

you're guaranteed to have more magical days than not so magical.

When you make this your lifestyle, even the not so magical days end up being magical, because they help you grow!

Trust me when I say this works, and it works extremely well. This will work no matter what your desire is. Whether you want to manifest a relationship, better health, more money, and a new job, whatever it may be- the morning dance will help get you there.

There have been a lot of social media challenges throughout the years. There was the infamous cinnamon challenge. There was the Drake In my Feelings challenge where people had to dance outside their car to that song.

~Have a Magical Day~

I'm officially issuing the Hope Nuggets Car Dance challenge. I challenge you to not only do the car dance in the morning but to post it on either your story or post feed and tag @hopenuggets. So get in your car, turn up the volume to your favorite song, and dance like no one is watching!

Let's start a car dance revolution! Let's start a high vibration, powerfully manifesting, hope inspired movement!

This will be so fun, and I cannot wait to see these posts. We're going to obliterate anxiety and depression one day at a time!

I guarantee that as you follow all the steps outlined in this book for your morning routine and top it

~Have a Magical Day~

off with your car dance, you will live happier, freer, healthier, and with tremendous success.

~Have a Magical Day~

I love you all! Thank you!!! #hopenuggets

#lovetheprocess #believeitandreceiveit

#haveamagicalday

~Have a Magical Day~

About the Author

Wendell Miracle is one of the world's most influential motivational speakers and is the founder of the internationally known Instagram page @hopenuggets. He started the page in 2013, recording fifteen-second videos. These short videos have touched lives all over the world.

~Have a Magical Day~

His goal is to help people overcome depression and anxiety through his teachings, videos, books, seminars, and social media reach. You can expect to see new & inspiring content on his Instagram page daily.

You can visit his website at www.hopenuggets.com and follow him on Instagram at www.instagram.com/hopenuggets

Made in USA - North Chelmsford, MA
1106349_9798605340454
05.14.2020 1509